THE
BEST CARTOONS
FROM

Collected for Americans
from England's Famous Humorous Weekly
Edited by Marvin Rosenberg and William Cole

SIMON AND SCHUSTER
1952

MANUFACTURED IN THE UNITED STATES OF AMERICA
LITHOGRAPHY BY THE MURRAY PRINTING COMPANY, WAKEFIELD, MASS.

Foreword

WHEREVER in this wide world my ship touches the shore, some kindly reporter asks the same silly question—generally at 6 o'clock in the morning when I am packing and cannot find my passport: "What, in your opinion, is the difference between English and American (Australian, Canadian, Argentinian, Egyptian, Ceylonese) humor?" I always answer: "There isn't any," which shocks them, I know not·why. Humor, to my mind, is one of the few earthly blessings about which there can be no claim to sovereign rights. "Man," wrote Hazlitt, in *The English Comic Writers*, "is the only animal that laughs and weeps, for he is the only animal that is struck by the difference between what things are and what they ought to be." There is, of course, another theory. A company of learned men, it is said, were discussing what was "the essence of humor"—what really made men laugh. Some said it was "incongruity," some said it was "misfortune," and some said this and that. A distinguished lawyer said: "Oh, no, the essence of humor is 'surprise': and that is why you laugh when you see a joke in *Punch*." But a friend of that paper said: "No. The essence of humor is 'recognition': and that is why you laugh if you hear a joke in court." (I tell you that story, by the way, in order to support the Briton's proud and famous claim that he is able to laugh at himself.) Incongruity—misfortune—surprise—recognition? Whatever the true theory, it applies, I fancy, to all men everywhere. The basic joke, perhaps the original joke, the dignified old gentleman in a top hat who slips up on a banana skin, will cause the same laughter in London or Lapland, Fifth Avenue or Fiji. Even the Russians would laugh at that: for the Russians have a sense of humor too, though now it may be illegal.

"Then why is it," says the smart reporter, "that Americans can gaze at a page of *Punch*, and Britons at a page of *The New Yorker*, not merely without a smile, but with a sense of amazed frustration, wondering how any magazine with comic ambitions could have come to publish a picture that provoked so little merriment? Surely the sense of humor is different?" No, it is the scene that is different. They would laugh in the jungle at the old gentleman and the banana skin, but not at jokes about motorcars, television or psychiatrists. We have psychiatrists too, but the breed is not so numerous or well-respected here; and some New York comments on their proceedings mystify many of us still.

The editors of this collection have wisely recognized this truth, and selected aspects of the human scene which are common to both nations. But there remain, of course, certain differences of emphasis. Our sense of humor may be the same weapon as the American, but we seem to use it in public, at least—what shall I say?—with more restraint?—more delicately?—just as American policemen are armed, and ours are not. For one thing, there are no "sexy" jokes or pictures here, nothing to compare, for example, with Peter Arno's famous couple in bed ("Wake up, you mutt. We're getting married today."). The nearest thing to a sexy joke that I can remember seeing in *Punch* was this: The Mayor of Liverpool, solemnly commemorating and confirming the long association of Liverpool with the River Mersey, threw a gold ring into the river. *Punch* said: "Now that Liverpool has been formally wedded to the Mersey, many are saying it is about time that Manchester did the right thing by the Ship Canal." *Punch* has always been aimed at the family, and not at Peter Arno's couple.

For the same reason, perhaps, we tend, I fancy, to be more kindly to mankind and its arrangements. Some comic artists seem to be obsessed by sex, domestic unhappiness, and a hatred for the human race. I love, and laugh aloud at many of them; but the cumulative effect is depressing to anyone who believes that the race already referred to has done a pretty good job and is, on the whole, worth preserving. All their men and women, old or young, are hideous; all married couples are always yelling at each other; and every man, it seems, is mentally undressing every woman he sees. It is fashionable in England now to sneer at the social "cartoons" in *Punch* of, say, 1860 or 1870. The jokes they illustrated may have been, to the lively taste of today, ponderous and wordy, as the clothes and customs, of course, are, to this great age, ridiculous. But the people are true and attractive: old people dignified, young people fine and handsome; if married couples disagreed, they disagreed politely; and their posterity are not ashamed to see them. If a theatrical manager wants to do a play about the '60's or '70's the first thing he does is to look up the old *Punch* volumes. There he sees exactly how our fathers spoke, and dressed, and looked. If the Cochran, or the Ziegfeld, of 2000 A.D. wants to do a play about 1952 A.D. I do not think he will get much help from the most popular comic artists of today. He will probably decide that the less said about his subhuman ancestors the better. But the main purpose of a comic artist, without doubt, is to be comic; and "If I do that," he may well say, "what are you complaining about?" Hastily, I agree, I accept, I withdraw. It was only an old chap maundering to himself. I salute this work and wish it well; and on behalf of *Punch* and his merry men may I proclaim their thanks for the compliment that America has paid them in supposing that Britain can be funny too.

A. P. Herbert

THERE IS only one good reason for an American to look at *Punch* cartoons—
they're *funny*. Funny in any country.
What American needs an introduction to the characters
in this little drama—

"*. . . and what's more he'll remain in the cellar
until he's in a more repentant frame of mind.*"

The British are the same kind of domestic animal we are.
British husbands have wives, and British wives have husbands—

"Here's a laugh, dear—'Provided his home is well run the
average man is unaware if his wife is in or not.'"

"Hello . . . Police? Well look here, there's
someone here reading the Daily Bugle and my
husband always reads the Daily Blah."

—and they eat breakfast together—

—though not always in peace—

In justice to British husbands,
they do sometimes make life easier for their spouses

though not always.

"Milk's boiling over!"

"How was I to know you were saving it for something?"

The British breadwinner,
like his American counterpart,
has a housing problem to face—

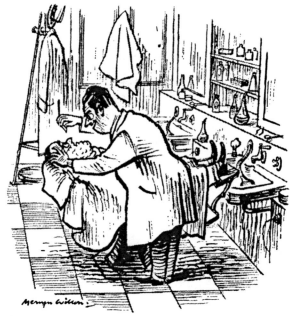

"I've heard a rumor that, with just a little persuasion, you might consider letting your flat."

"Of course we are prepared to make one or two small alterations for suitable tenants."

which he meets
with sturdy inventiveness.

*"Father hasn't said anything yet but
I think he feels it's time we got
a car of our own."*

Like us, the British must cope with furniture, old . . .

and new . . .

and rugs, large . . .

"Don't trouble. I've found it."

and small . . .

and television, which gives the usual trouble . . .

"I didn't think it would end like this."

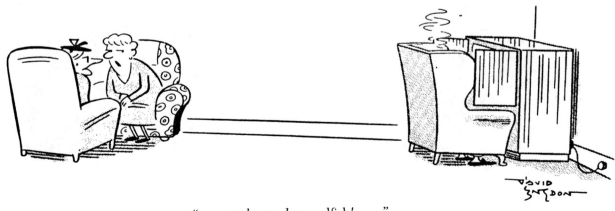

". . . and, my dear, selfish! . . ."

in all sorts of places . . .

"But Sir Bedivere always walks the battlements at this hour. Can't think what's keeping him."

to all sorts of individuals.

Britons entertain at dinner . . .

"Thank you for a really wonderful evening, Mrs. Soames. So stupid of me to forget I mustn't touch crab."

play games . . .

and go to contemporary art shows . . .

"One misses a lot—being brought up to appreciate it."

go to business . . .

where they have secretaries . . .

"Dear Sirs . . . A squiggly bit with a circle, followed by a couple of dots, a thing like a worm, then a sort of hairpin on its side . . ."

"Why, Mr. Smith! What on earth are you doing in the 'M' file?"

"Why are all the letters different?"

and suggestion boxes . . .

"That's fine, R.B., but wouldn't it be a trifle more adventurous to have a slot made in it?"

and office problems.

"Sometimes I think it will drive me mad."

British traffic moves down the left-hand side of the street,
but women drivers are exactly the same . . .

"Steady, steady! Pull over to the landing-stage! Left, left! Slow
down!"

"Avoid loose stones and watch out for that
Brontosaurus round the corner."

English traffic is cluttered with busses that have
unmistakable bus habits . . .

*The brakes on some of the new busses are, I
think, just a shade—*

fiercer than before—

but then, if it comes to that—

so are their clutches.

Whenever you see an "L" on a license plate
you have fair warning that the driver is learning . . .

whenever you see it.

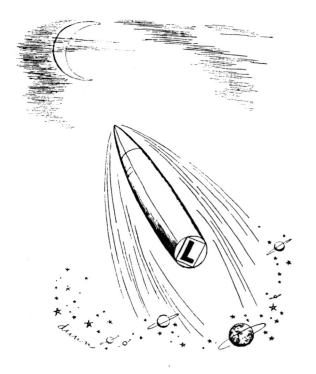

Sidewalk artists and entertainers are more common
in England than in America . . .

but everyone knows what a sandwich man looks like . . .

or a street vendor . . .

"'Ere we go again—the State versus Free Enterprise."

The British have had more than their share of shortages . . .

of many kinds . . .

"Ordered a new car six years ago, and it's just arrived. Not quite the model I specified . . ."

"Air, water, and a piece of string, please."

and can still laugh about them . . .

"May we have our tomato back?"

albeit somewhat wryly.

*"To let you see how it would look on you
abroad, sir."*

*"Try to think of something that
doesn't require dollars."*

And for all these familiar problems,
and the legion of others they share with us,
the British, too, have that ultimate in modern conveniences—
the psychiatrist.

*"Will my husband leave me for the other woman?—Will my homicidal tendencies
develop?—Don't miss next week's thrilling consultation."*

"... and always, I feel that I'm an awful bore."

By now you may have begun to recognize the unique styles
of some of the artists, so let us introduce you formally.
For instance, the great *Emett,*
whose crazy world often seems so much saner
than our own . . .

*". . . and a rather neat arrangement with the County Council takes care of the
expenses of my walking tour."*

and the incomparable *Sprod,*

who is particularly apt with statuary in distress . . .

Anton, whose sympathies often run to villains, counterfeiters, and similar misunderstood persons . . .

Geo. M. draws a world of long ago . . .

"But I can't get a baby sitter—they won't come where there isn't a jester."

Whereas it's doubtful whether
André Francois' fantastic world and people ever existed . . .

Hollowood's characters are among those you'll encounter most frequently in this volume . . .

"*Hurry up, dear, your breakfast cereal's barely audible.*"

and *frolik*'s

"Sir—I have used the same safety razor blade for 253 consecutive days. Is this a record?"

and *Mahood*'s

and *Scully*'s.

Taylor's genial style is unmistakable . . .

and so are *ffolkes'* folks.

"I just can't do arms."

And you'll be sure to spot the work of *Brockbank*

"I'll stay in here till you come, dear. There's a man outside who frightens me."

and *Wiles*

and *Siggs*

and *Dunn*

"Perhaps it was her maiden name."

and *Ionicus*

and *Graham*

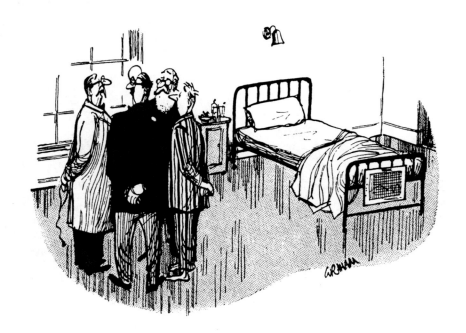

and *Starke*

and many others you'll meet as you go along. Have fun!

"Are you sure we brought him?"

"Just sits there toying with her food."

"Now to start with, let's make a list of all the famous and important men who were short."

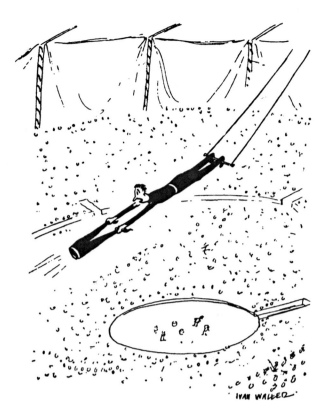

"*Marjorie!*"

"*We're hoping that one day he'll remember his errand and go off as mysteriously as he came.*"

"Do you mind if I sit in front of the French horns tonight? I've just had my hair cut."

"Usual guff about a bearded stranger."

"I forgot the salt."

"Of course, I only breed them for the brandy."

*". . . yet how is it these vital facts are virtually unknown in this
country today?"*

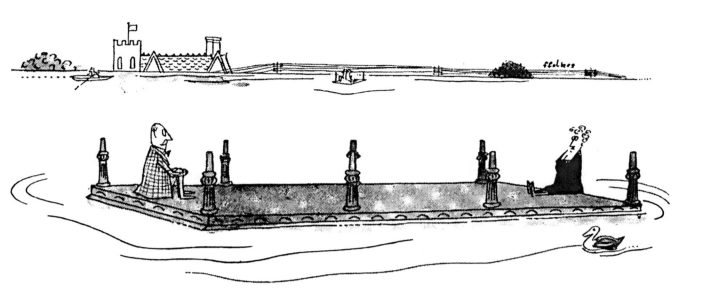

"There, what did I say? I arrive here every day at 10:12 A.M. precisely, and precisely at 10:12 A.M. every day he slams the thing in my face."

"I said, 'No one would ever take you for sixty-six.'"

". . . and I ask, gentlemen, if this is the face of a villain, a cheat and a parasite?"

"Of course, it's the people that can remove these things that really make the big money."

"And another thing—you'll have to stop him drawing all over the walls."

"*Some oaf's carved on the great oak tree, proper, two hearts conjoined in fess, charged respectively with the letters A H and E F and transfixed with an arrow, also in fess, barbed and feathered pointing sinister; all surmounted in chief by the figures 1, 9, 5 and 0. And for the legend, displayed without a label, 'Alf loves Emmie.'*"

"You are very, very lucky to be able
to weigh yourself at prewar
prices. . . ."

"Warm, warm . . ."

"There's definitely something wrong with that machine!"

"Let's see, just how long is it since we started this picture?"

"I joined the Legion two or three weeks ago to try to forget a girl called Elsie or something."

'Of course, for the last twenty years
we've had to help him up.'

Andri François

"Seen my collar, Mildred?"

"Surely they ought to fit this cage with smaller mesh."

*"This will make them think either that we had a
ladder, or else that the floor subsided."*

"My husband's no good as an electrician, but he's terribly clever at carpentry."

THE STORY OF MANKIND

"Here—in spite of snow, sleet, frost, and biting winds—are the Thompsons."

"Somehow I couldn't discard him completely."

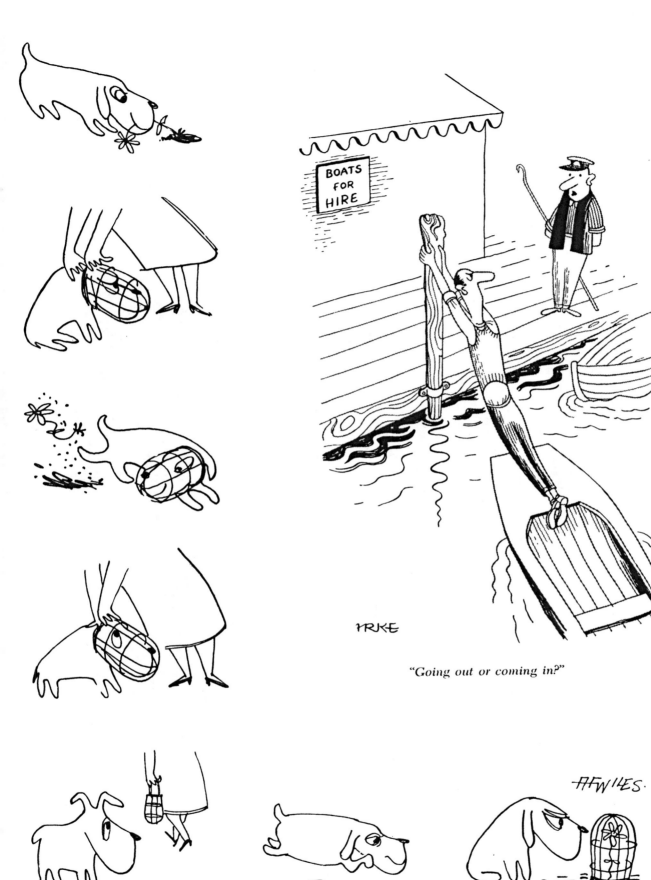

"Going out or coming in?"

"We hesitated a long time before installing a lift, but fortunately it's Period. . . ."

"Do you mind if my friend just takes it into the daylight?"

"Yes, quite a good house dog."

"I'd better come back when you've made up your mind."

"Yes, certainly. What sort of favor?"

"I had such a nightmare last night—got knocked out at Rugger and my MOTHER rushed on the field to help me."

"Any more for the Roman Villa . . . ?"

"Pvpry timp I strikp thp lpttpr 'p' I gpt an 'e'."

"Now add the sugar."   *"Now add the sugar"* . . .   *"Now add the sugar"* . . .

"And this is a record of him cutting his first tooth."

"Just our luck! They would take us alphabetically!"

"And how's the old claustrophobia this morning, Sir Charles?"

"Fortunately I was able to get his likeness before he ran away."

"No, I don't think one would suit you!"

"Yes, Fido is just like one of the family."

"Your change, sir!"

"It's the sitter-in; she can't come."

"By Jove—that was a narrow escape."

"Tell you when the tightrope act's over; tell you when the trapeze act's over; tell you when the lion-tamer-in-the-lion's-mouth act's over. Waste of money bringing you along."

"It seems funny, when you remember that actually we're going the other way."

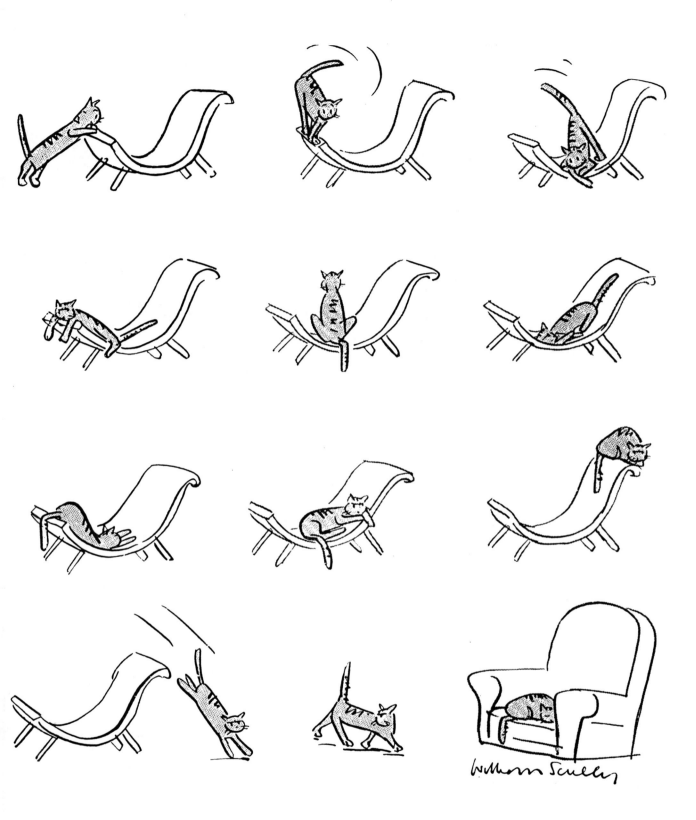

"I suppose it's psychoneurosis, but I've got an awful feeling of something nasty creeping up on me."

"It says here, 'During mock battles the utmost economy in ammunition will be observed . . .'"

"ANOTHER *complaint*, Rogers?"

"Who does it turn out to be?"

"Why, Mrs. Johnson, I hoped you were going to bring your little
boy with you again."

"Pemberton's the most persuasive speaker I've
ever met."

"I was wondering whether I might possibly
transfer to a room with a slightly smaller key?"

"That reminds me, dear—did you remember the sandwiches?"

"By the way, dear, I've fixed that drawer so it doesn't stick any more."

"Good gracious! The water must be filthy."

"Would everybody kindly pay attention and note that I am
about to purchase a paper by putting down a sixpenny piece and
taking five pennies change?"

"How's it done? Whichever one I point to he opens and it's empty."

"Those? Oh, games were compulsory."

DonWait

"For my next illusion, I shall need the help of one of those inveterate exhibitionists whose sole desire in life appears to be that of aiding stage performers such as myself."

Hewison

"I believe he's standing on his head again."

"On the other hand, I hardly feel that being sorry for you is a sufficiently solid foundation for a happy marriage."

"So we bought a couple of hens and I was to write a humorous best seller about our misfortunes—but it didn't work out."

"Good heavens, Lavinia! It says here the East Wing was burned down last night."

"It's quite nice, but the noise in the afternoons is almost unbearable!"

"I said 'Push me the sugar!'"

"And don't say 'Oh, what a noble mind is here o'erthrown' every time your father opens his mouth, or I'll stop you going to the pictures altogether."

"Someone ought to stop us before we get hurt."

"That's another of my labor-saving devices—which one, I can't remember."

"Well, funnily enough, at first it did cross our minds that he might have escaped from somewhere."

"How strange! We're friends of the author too."

"Yes, yes, no, yes, yes, no, no, yes, no, yes, thank you."

PATENTS
OFFICE

"His blood ran cold as he saw the sinister round blue eyes and pink face of Johnny Jones staring at him over the window sill."

"I THOUGHT fifteen miles was too long for the cross-country race."

"Listen, George, they are playing our
tune."

". . . and Mrs. Jack Sprat, of course, was merely endeavoring to correct a
vitamin B deficiency."

"I'm an Egyptologist; what's your racket?"

"I think he's beginning to notice girls."

*"I know what they're thinking. They're thinking what a shabby
old saucepan to let a boy get his head stuck into."*

*"One of the cardinal rules of smash and grab is: Pinch a vehicle that'll keep the
hue and cry at a distance. . . ."*

"And if you want anything, just ring."

WILARKE.

"He won them for something or other."

"... and since you are the 499,999th visitor to our Festival Year show, we should like you to accept ..."

"What's the use of fighting it, darling? This thing is bigger than both of us."

"I'm sorry I ever mentioned that he had a stone in his hoof."

"Run along child, and try to play."

"I paint what I see, child."

"I just don't seem to be hungry."

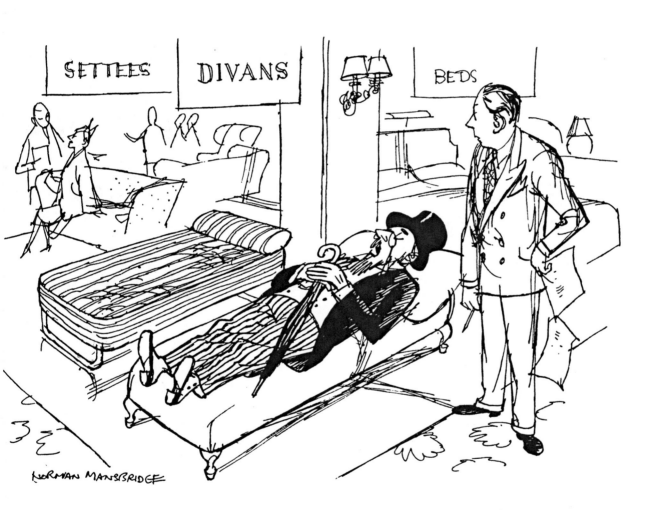

"Yes. This will suit my patients very well. The truth is, I am a psychiatrist.
Born in the early summer of 1884, just outside Vienna, I remember how my
stepfather . . ."

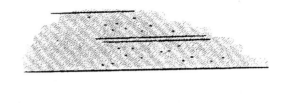

"Pardon me. Do you happen to have seen a man carrying a suitcase marked 'Belloni and his Talking Dog'? . . ."

"Stand by for whipping away the marmalade and substituting the coffeepot!"

"Is there any evidence to support this rumor that one of the cleaners has won thirty thousand in a football pool?"

"Isn't there ANYTHING we mustn't do?"

"But, darling, it makes you look thirty years younger!"

"Garçon, la multiplication, s'il vous plaît."

"Well, there's nothing much wrong
with this lamp."

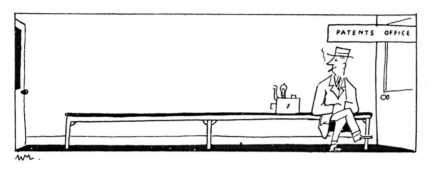

VOTE FOR
PERKINS
THE
FORTHRIGHT
CANDIDATE

Punchiana

THE first issue of *Punch* made its modest appearance on July 17, 1841, and sold two editions of 5,000 each. The capital of the promoters was £25, or approximately $100. The first Almanack (Winter Double Number) was published the following year, and the circulation jumped in one week from 6,000 to 90,000! The Almanack was thought up by H. P. Grattan while in a debtors' prison, aided by another staff member, Henry Mayhew, who lived secretly in the prison for a week. The two men are said to have produced thirty-five jokes a day for seven days.

*　　*　　*

THE first editor was Mark Lemon, and at an early meeting someone spoke of the proposed publication as being like a good mixture of punch, nothing without Lemon. That is how *Punch* got its name. In 111 years *Punch* has had only seven editors. Lemon held the post for 29 years. Shirley Brooks and Tom Taylor had short editorships covering the next decade, and then Sir Francis Burnand took over for the years from 1880–1906. Sir Owen Seaman headed the staff from 1906–1932, and E. V. Knox from 1932–1949. The present Editor, Kenneth Bird, is better known to cartoon enthusiasts as "Fougasse," and he is the first artist ever to hold the position.

*　　*　　*

THE editorial staff carry on a century-old tradition of meeting weekly round the famous *Punch* table, which is inscribed with the initials of *Punch* staffs back to 1855. Over a meal, ideas are conceived for the next issue. Only one American has ever been present at this ceremony—Mark Twain.

*　　*　　*

W. M. THACKERAY, Lord Tennyson and W. S. Gilbert wrote for *Punch* in the Victorian era. Charles Dickens had work rejected!

*　　*　　*

W. S. GILBERT asked Burnand if many jokes were sent in. "Hundreds," said Burnand. "Why don't you print some of them?" was the rejoinder.

*　　*　　*

IT WAS Burnand who replied, "It never was," to the famous and oft-repeated remark, "*Punch* is not as good as it was."

*　　*　　*

DURING the Fuel Crisis in 1947 *Punch*, for the first time in its history, failed to appear. Continuity was maintained through the courtesy of *The Times*, which published the principal cartoons from the two missing issues.

*　　*　　*

ALTHOUGH chiefly known as a humorous magazine, *Punch* has always wielded a lively political and crusading pen and pencil. In the last century it was banned three times from France and once from the Court of the Emperor of Germany. The Emperor, however, continued to receive his copy in a sealed envelope with the official mail from London. *Punch* first achieved international fame with the publication of "The Song of the Shirt," a tragic poem by Thomas Hood on the plight of underpaid seamstresses. The effect of its publication in 1843 was tremendous, and the poem was translated into every European language.

Printed in the United States
128861LV00001B/51/A

9 780548 387450